I0605356

I CAN BE A WRITER

I Can Be a Book Author

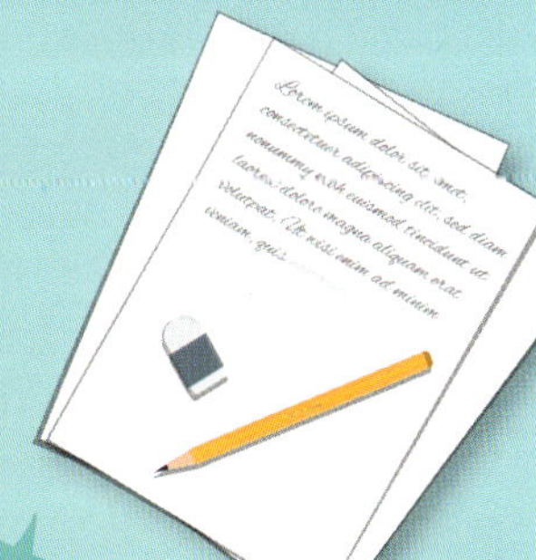

Meeg Pincus

Published in the United States of America by:

CHERRY LAKE PRESS
2395 South Huron Parkway, Suite 200, Ann Arbor, Michigan 48104
www.cherrylakepress.com

Reading Adviser: Beth Walker Gambro, MS, Ed., Reading Consultant, Yorkville, IL

Photo Credits: © Cherry Lake Publishing Group, 5; © Wisconsinart/Dreamstime.com, 6; © VectorMine / Shutterstock, 7; © Sleeping Bear Press, used with permission, 8 (left), 8 (right); © hamdi bendali/Shutterstock, 9; © Wavebreakmedia Ltd/Dreamstime.com, 11; © Constantin Opris/Dreamstime.com, 12; © Lamai Prasitsuwan/ Shutterstock, 13; © Dwong19/Dreamstime.com, 14; © Markus Wissmann/Shutterstock, 15; © wavebreakmedia/ Shutterstock, 16; © Rapeepat Pornsipak/Shutterstock, 18; © wavebreakmedia/Shutterstock, 20; © IZZ HAZEL/ Shutterstock, 21; © patpitchaya/Shutterstock, 22

Copyright © 2026 by Cherry Lake Publishing Group

All rights reserved. No part of this book may be reproduced or utilized in any form or by any means without written permission from the publisher.

Cherry Lake Press is an imprint of Cherry Lake Publishing Group.

Library of Congress Cataloging-in-Publication Data has been filed and is available at catalog.loc.gov

Cherry Lake Publishing Group would like to acknowledge the work of the Partnership for 21st Century Learning, a Network of Battelle for Kids. Please visit Battelle for Kids online for more information.

Printed in the United States of America

Note from publisher: Websites change regularly, and their future contents are outside of our control. Supervise children when conducting any recommended online searches for extended learning opportunities.

CONTENTS

WHAT DO BOOK AUTHORS DO?

Do you love to have someone read a great book to you? Do you like to read past your bedtime? Is there a favorite book you've wanted to read again and again?

Then you have seen what book authors do!

Book authors write the text, or words, of a book. They may write books for children, teenagers, or adults.

Children's books come in many shapes and sizes. Each book has an author.

Some book authors write fiction. They use their imagination to make up a story and characters. They may create a new world or set their story in a real place.

Fiction stories may include talking animals and magical worlds.

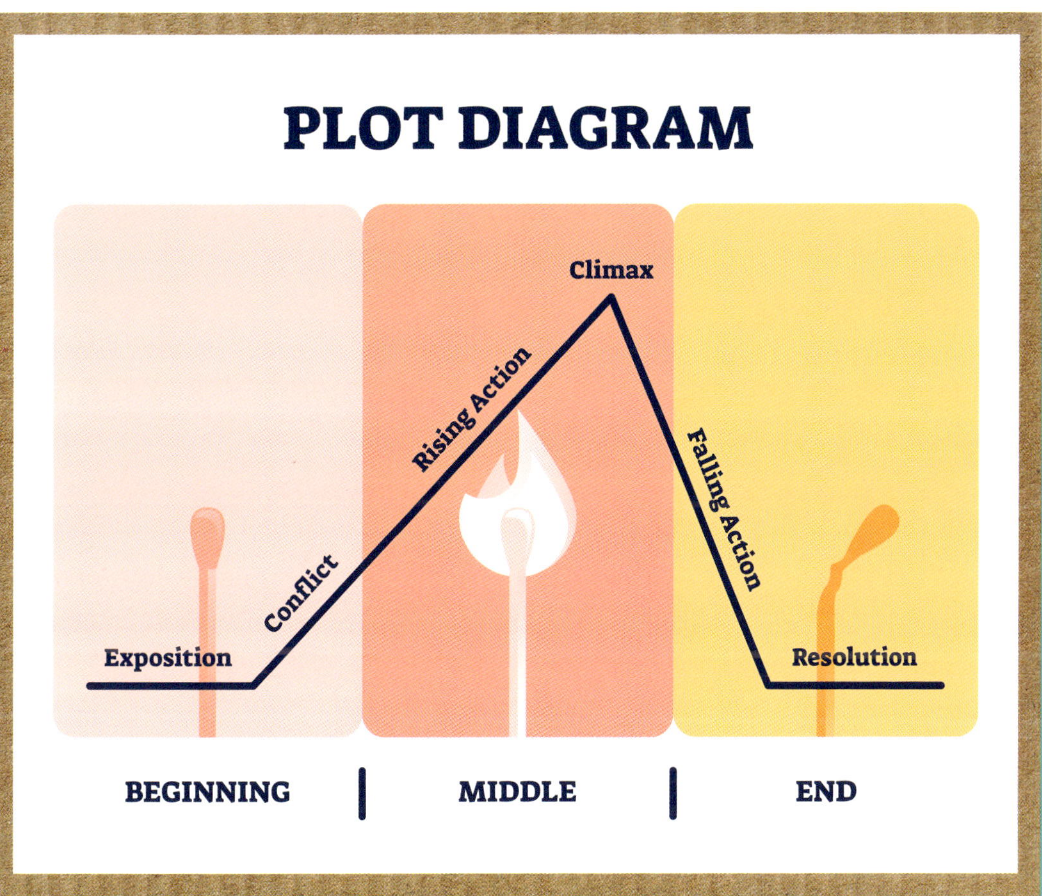

Fiction authors craft a **plot** for each book they write. They write a beginning, middle, and end. They create drama for their characters to keep readers turning pages.

Some book authors write nonfiction. Their books are based on facts and true stories.

Most nonfiction authors do a lot of research. They learn all they can about a topic before they write. They may read articles and books, interview people, or watch films.

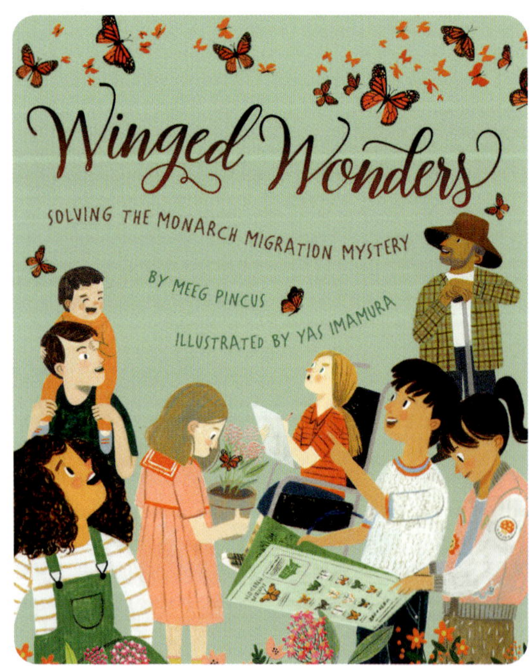

Other nonfiction authors write about their own real-life stories. This kind of book is called a **memoir** or autobiography.

Think!

What do your favorite books have in common? Are they fiction or nonfiction? Are they set in real or imaginary places?

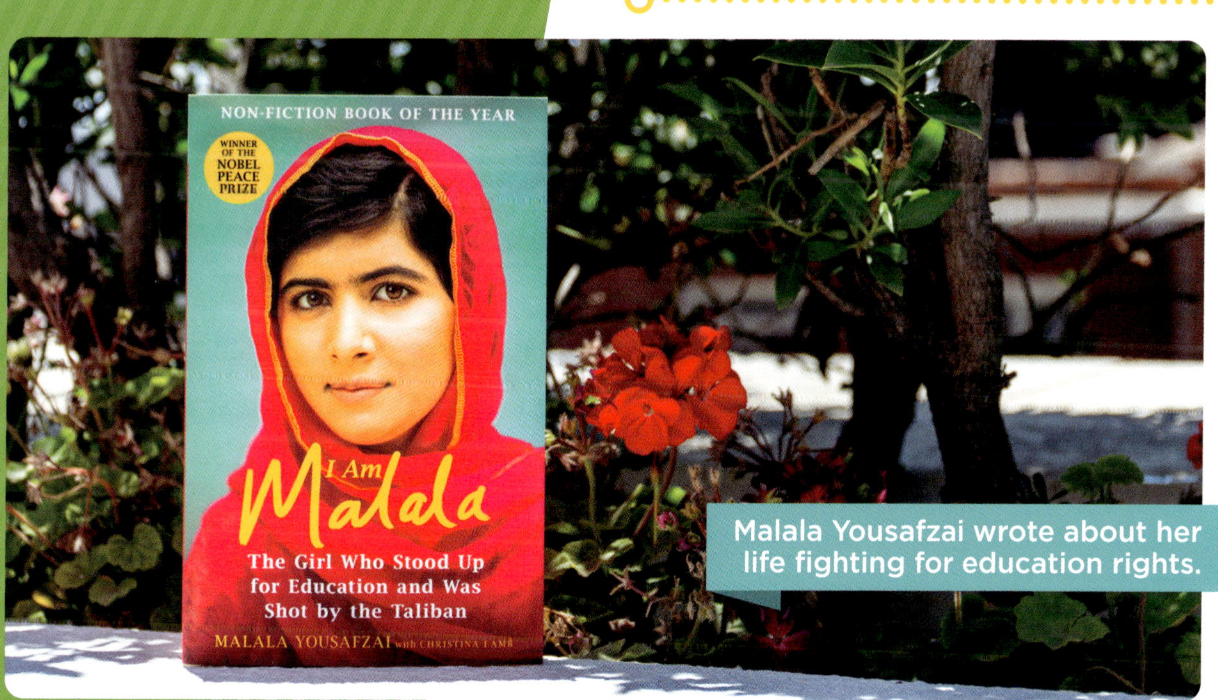

Malala Yousafzai wrote about her life fighting for education rights.

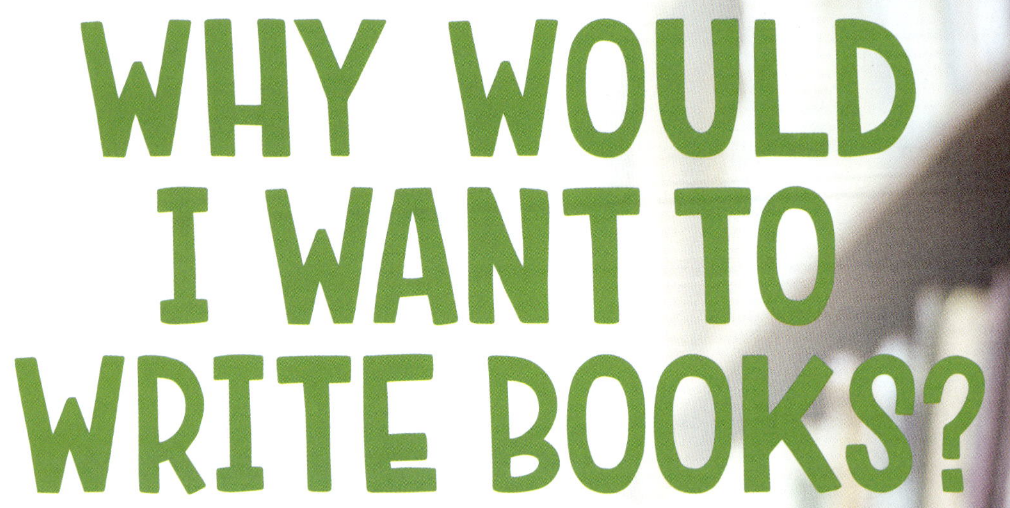

WHY WOULD I WANT TO WRITE BOOKS?

Do you often imagine stories or topics you want to write about? Is going to the library or bookstore fun for you? Are you excited by the idea of writing words someone may read again and again?

Then you may want to write books!

Create!

Keep a journal listing the books you've read. Write down what you liked or didn't like about each book, plus any ideas it sparked. Notice your patterns over time.

Some authors like a neat, quiet space to write in. Some prefer clutter and noise.

Being a book author means spending a lot of time by yourself. If you like to be alone to imagine, think, research, and write, you may enjoy writing books.

Make a Guess!

What do you think it means to say, "Writing is rewriting"? How much do you think authors need to revise their manuscripts before they become books?

Book authors also write many **drafts** of each book. They get **feedback** from **editors** and others. They work to improve their **manuscript** before it can become a book.

To be a book author, you live by the saying, "Writing is rewriting."

Do you like the idea of reading your book to an audience at a bookstore, school, or library? Would you enjoy talking to others about your writing?

Book authors also work to **promote** their books to readers. If you enjoy being in a community of book people, this may be a path for you.

Author events can involve signing books, meeting fans, and reading your book to an audience.

HOW CAN I LEARN TO WRITE BOOKS?

How many books have you read this month? Book authors are also book readers!

Go to the library and check out books that interest you. Ask for books as gifts. The more books you read, the better writer you will become.

Keep a writing notebook with you. Jot down story and plot ideas as you think of them.

Becoming a book author takes many years of writing practice. Just like reading books, the more you write, the better writer you will become.

You can write your own stories and books for practice. Try writing in different **styles** and lengths. Try writing fiction and nonfiction. Write often!

Look!

When you are at the library or bookstore, notice what book covers interest you. Do you like bright or dark, detailed or simple book covers? Do they match the kinds of stories you like to write?

What kind of book would you like to write?

You can take classes in fiction and nonfiction writing. You can join writing groups where people share their writing and feedback with each other. You can enter writing contests.

Can you be a book author? If you want to learn to write imagined or true stories for people to read as books . . . yes, you can!

ACTIVITY

Choose a favorite book.

Study how the book is written. Ask yourself:

- Does the author use long or short sentences?
- Is there more description or more **dialogue**?
- Do they write in the voice of one of the story's characters or an **outside narrator**?

Then write your own story using the style you discovered. Mimic the author's way of telling a story. You can use their characters and setting or create your own.

See what you learn from writing like a real book author!

FIND OUT MORE

Books

DK. *Write Your Own Book.* New York, NY: DK Publishing, 2016.

Haidle, Elizabeth. *Before They Were Authors: Famous Writers as Kids.* New York, NY: Houghton Mifflin Harcourt, 2019.

Websites

With an adult, explore more online with these suggested searches.

Book Club for Kids podcast, where kids talk with book authors

"Meet the Authors Movie Collection," *Teaching Books*

"Writers Speak to Kids" video series, *NBC News*

ABOUT THE AUTHOR

Meeg Pincus loves to write. She is the author of more than 30 books for children. She has been a writer and editor for books, newspapers, magazines, and more. She also loves to sing, make art, and hang out with her family, friends, and adorable dog.

GLOSSARY

dialogue **(DYE-uh-lawg)** conversation between characters

drafts **(DRAFTS)** early versions of a piece of writing

editors **(EH-duh-ters)** people who help prepare or improve a piece of writing

feedback **(FEED-bak)** comments, opinions, or corrections

manuscript **(MAN-yuh-skript)** text or draft of a book before it is published

memoir **(MEM-wahr)** story about a person's life from their perspective

outside narrator **(owt-SIYD NAIR-ay-ter)** storyteller speaking from outside of the story, not as a character in it

plot **(PLAHT)** series of events that make up a story

promote **(pruh-MOHT)** help introduce or sell a product

revise **(ree-VIEZ)** make changes

styles **(STIE-uhls)** ways in which something is done, created, or performed

INDEX